Youth Sports

Winning Strategies for Parent Coaches

Table of Contents

Chapter 1. Introduction

Welcome to our Special Report "Youth Sports: Winning Strategies for Parent Coaches"! This extraordinary resource is your ticket to creating a positive, enriching, and fun sporting experience for our young athletes. Filled with practical strategies and valuable tips from seasoned coaches and sports psychologists, we unravel the secrets of effective coaching. This report offers you insights into fostering team spirit, encouraging individual growth, and setting your young team up for success while ensuring they enjoy the ride. Celebrate the world of sports with us, make every practice count, and guide our future champions beyond winning and losing. Don't miss the chance to transform your coaching journey while making a lasting impact on these budding athletes' lives!

Chapter 2. Understanding the Role of a Parent Coach

To understand the role of a parent coach is to delve into the very heart of youth sports. This journey is a dynamic one, full of unique responsibilities and chances to make a difference every day. It truly goes beyond the play field and into the realm of early-stage character building and life mentoring. Let's break this down.

2.1. The Dynamics of Double Roles

The role of a parent coach is a dual one, and this comes with its own intricacies. It involves being both a mentor and a guardian, a coach and a parent, responsible for not just sporting performance, but also the holistic development of the child.

In many instances, parent coaches find themselves combating dual expectations from their children, which can be complex. As a coach, you're sought for expertise, guidance, and strategies related to the sport. However, as a parent, you are sought for emotional comfort, understanding, and unwavering support. Balancing these roles effectively is the keystone of your success.

In this dual role, you are dealing with an athlete on the field and your child at home, and it's crucial not to blur these boundaries. On the field, all players should be treated equally, without favoritism. At home, your child deserves the same support and attention as if they were not part of your team.

2.2. Building a Positive Sporting Environment

At the heart of cultivating a youth team is creating a positive sporting environment. This positivity should permeate all aspects of the sport - the play, the players, and especially the ethos of the team. Your main goal should be to foster an environment that encourages fun, teamwork, respect, and perseverance.

A golden rule to remember is that the game is, after all, a game. It's crucial to create an atmosphere where winning is encouraged but not seen as the only form of success. Instead, each player's personal development and contribution to the team spirit should be equally celebrated.

Promote a sense of belonging in the team. When your young players feel that they are integral parts of the group, they learn to value their teammates, and that leads to improved teamwork and unity.

2.3. Echoing Sportsmanship

As a parent coach, you're uniquely positioned to nurture an attitude of sportsmanship in your team. The values you live by will determine your team's character. Promote a sense of fairness and respect, not just for their teammates, but also towards opponents.

Teaching your athletes the importance of gracious winning and losing is vital. Help them understand that losing is not a failure, rather an opportunity to learn, improve, and become stronger, and winning is not a destination, but one of the many milestones in their sporting journey.

2.4. Individual Growth and Skills Development

As a coach, your role goes beyond just team victories on the field. You're tasked with the imperative responsibility of your children's individual skill growth. This means understanding the strengths and weaknesses of each player and then tailoring instruction and advice accordingly.

Identify specific development areas for each child to ensure their continuous growth. This could be in athletic ability, the understanding of the game, or mental toughness. Remember, early on, emphasis should be placed more on skill development rather than competition alone.

2.5. Communication: The Vital Bridge

Effective communication is the foundation of any successful coach-player relationship. It's essential to keep the lines of communication open with your children, both as players and as your kids. Clear, honest, and open conversations about objectives, room for improvements, and future plans make your young athletes feel valued and understood.

Moreover, communication extends beyond just your team. Connecting with other parents, referees, coaching staff, and sometimes even opponents, is a large part of a coach's role.

2.6. The Mental and Emotional Aspect

Last but not least, be mindful of your athletes' mental and emotional well-being. The world of sports can be challenging, and it's your responsibility to guide your team through these trials.

Maintain a balanced perspective. Celebrations, disappointments, wins, losses—they are all part of the game, and you need to help them navigate these experiences. Encourage them to set realistic, yet challenging goals and assist them on that journey.

In conclusion, the role of a parent coach is a complex and nuanced one. Yet, it comes with incredible rewards – the chance to shape, nurture, and meaningfully contribute to the development of our future champions. Your journey as a parent coach is sure to be enriching and rewarding as you embolden these young athletes, inspire their dreams, and walk side by side with them in their sporting endeavors. So, put on that coach's cap, step onto the field, and let's make a difference, one game at a time.

Chapter 3. The Psychology of Youth Sports: Building Resilience

Engaging in sports serves as an excellent platform for children not only for physical development but also for acquiring critical psychological skills. Most paramount among these is resilience, a quality that allows children to encounter, stand up to, and recover from challenging situations, both on the playing field and off it.

3.1. Understanding Resilience in Youth Sports

Resilience can be defined as the capacity to recover quickly from difficulties; it's a form of toughness. In the context of youth sports, we consider resilience as the ability to endure setbacks, deal with defeat, and keep working towards goals irrespective of obstacles. Training resilience, often mistaken merely for enduring hard times, is a complex process that requires sensitively helping young athletes to maintain motivation, take calculated risks and learn from errors.

3.2. Cultivating Resilience

Building resilience in young athletes should be a priority for every parent and coach. The attributes that make up resilience, such as perseverance, adaptability, and optimism, are as essential as any physical skill in sports - and beyond.

1. Developing a Positive Mindset: Encourage athletes to focus on their preparation and effort instead of the results. Teach them to view setbacks as opportunities to learn and grow, and not as

personal failures.

2. Building Strong Relationships: Support from friends, family, and teammates can significantly impact an athlete's resilience. Foster a sense of community within the team and encourage open and honest communication.

3. Fostering Adaptability: Athletes need to understand that change is an inherent part of life and sports. They have to learn to adapt to different situations, expectations, and roles on the team, all of which foster resilience.

4. Setting Achievable Goals: Assist young athletes in setting realistic but challenging short-term and long-term goals. Achieving these targets can build self-confidence, a critical aspect of resilience.

3.3. Emotional Intelligence & Resilience

Equipping youth with emotional intelligence can play a significant role in fostering resilience. Emotional intelligence involves recognizing and managing personal emotions and the emotions of those around them. With emotional intelligence, youth athletes can manage the highs and lows that come with sports more effectively. They could develop empathy towards their teammates' feelings and bond better as a team, leading to the development of a support system that bolsters psychological resilience.

3.4. The Coach's Role in Building Resilience

As a coach, your job is not just teaching the technical aspects of the sport, but also working on building up these young athletes mentally and emotionally. One of the ways of doing this is through nourishing their resilience.

1. Encourage Failure: This might seem counter-intuitive, but one way to build resilience is to encourage failure — or rather, to encourage athletes to view failure differently. Frame failures as opportunities to learn and grow, and not as the end-all of their sporting journey.

2. Persistence Promotion: For resilience to be developed, young athletes must learn to keep pushing on, no matter how hard things get. They need to learn the art of continuing in the face of adversity.

3. Emotional Support: Being there for your young athletes emotionally will go a long way in building resilience. Allow them safe spaces to express their emotions and concerns.

3.5. Nurturing Resilience in Practice

It's not just about what you teach them. It's also about what you enable them to practice. Creating scenarios during training that develop resilience can be extremely beneficial.

1. Scrimmage Games: A controlled game situation can be an excellent place for athletes to experience the thrill of victory and the agony of defeat in a controlled, educational environment. Responding to the defeat and then trying to win can encourage resilient qualities in the athletes.

2. Role Play: This can be a great tool for working on resilience. Athletes can be given different roles within the team for certain practices or drills. This allows them to adapt to new roles, thus developing flexibility and resilience.

3. Challenging Drills: Select drills that are hard but achievable for your athletes. When they accomplish them, they build their self-confidence, which can boost resilience.

Remember, resilience isn't built in a day. Patience is key when cultivating this critical life skill, and the benefits will last a lifetime, both on and off the field. With persistence in teaching and nurturing, you will find your young athlete navigating bumps on their sporting journey with much more assurance, grace, and effectiveness.

Chapter 4. Involving Parents: The Balancing Act

As the coach, you hold an important position that allows you to shape the sporting experience for the young players under your care. A significant component of this is how you interact and involve the parents of your young athletes. Striking a right balance in the involvement of parents can be likened to performing a graceful balancing act, teetering between control and delegation, discipline and flexibility, guidance and freedom.

4.1. Establishing a Robust Communication System

Effective communication acts as the bedrock of a good relationship between parent-coaches and parents. It plays a key role in setting clear expectations, mitigating possible conflicts, and promoting a conducive environment for the young athletes.

Creating a robust communication system does not need to be a complex process. Simple strategies like sharing a seasonal calendar with practices, games, and important events can enhance clarity. Regular emails or briefings can keep everyone on the same page and foster a sense of community. A good rule of thumb is to keep the lines of communication clear and open, be reachable, and approachable. Encourage parents to share concerns or suggestions promptly, and ensure you respond in a constructive manner.

4.2. Draw the Boundary Lines

While the parents' involvement is necessary, it is also crucial to draw the boundary lines to ensure a conducive and distraction-free environment for the children. Formulating and enforcing a code of conduct can be effective in managing parental behavior during practices and matches. This code should have clear and reasonable boundaries regarding behavior on and off the field, emphasizing respect for all players, coaches, and officials.

Such boundary lines can help alleviate the pressure on the youngsters, contributing positively to their overall sporting experience. Reinforce these guidelines continuously throughout the season to remind parents of their integral role in creating a conducive environment for their children's growth.

4.3. Encouraging Positive Participation

There are numerous ways parents can be actively involved without causing disruptions. Encourage parents to become team moms or dads, helping out with snacks, fundraising, or match organization. Not only does this foster an environment of community and teamwork, but it also helps lighten the logistical load on the coach's shoulders.

4.4. Navigating the Tricky Terrain of Parental Concerns

Staying open to parental feedback while maintaining the boundaries can be a tough line to walk. A transparent approach can be advisable here, listening to each parent's concerns while also reminding them of the bigger picture. Establishing regular feedback sessions, either one-on-one or as a group, can help manage these concerns before they snowball.

4.5. Emphasizing Skill Development Above Winning

As a coach, you carry the significant responsibility of setting the tone for the sporting pursuit. Parents need constant reassurance that skill development and enjoyment are far more valuable than winning at this stage. Regularly share updates on each child's development, focusing on areas of improvement rather than just wins or losses. This also helps shift parental conversation at home, reinforcing the same values you instill during coaching.

4.6. Conflict Resolution Strategies

There might be times when you find yourself in the middle of heated discussions or disagreements. Handling these can be challenging, but with a structured conflict resolution approach, you can navigate these situations efficiently. The key is to address the issue at hand rather than the person and avoid emotional reactions.

Finally, throughout this balancing act, remember that your primary responsibility rests with the players - the children who love the game and look up to you for guidance and coaching. As a coach, your perspective can shape their sports experience, and the influence you bear on them is profound. With effective parental involvement strategies, you can play your part in creating an enriching and fulfilling journey in the world of sports for all involved.

Chapter 5. Effective Communication Strategies for Young Athletes

Effective communication is essential to create a supportive, productive, and dynamic team environment. For young athletes, understanding the importance of open, positive, and respectful conversation can lead to better performance, stronger relationships, and a deeper love for the sport. It is crucial to understand that while they may be young, athletes are also learners and are aware of the nuances that influence their engagement and progress in sports.

5.1. The Importance of Communication in Youth Sports

At its core, communication is the sharing of information, be it ideas, feelings, or instructions. Sports, especially team sports, rely heavily on effective communication both on and off the field. As a coach of young athletes, your communication abilities can significantly impact how your teammates comprehend their roles, take instructions, and implement feedback.

Moreover, your relationship with your young athletes strengthens when you communicate well. You can use different communication techniques to build trust, inspire, motivate, and guide your team. A coach who emphasizes clear, precise, and positive communication nurtures a team culture that promotes mutual respect, understanding, positivity, and determination.

5.2. Enhancing Your Verbal Communication Skills

Effective verbal communication is the linchpin of coaching. Below are some strategies to improve your verbal communication skills:

1. Be clear and concise: Your instructions should be clear and easy to understand. Avoid using jargon or complex terms that might confuse young athletes.

2. Use positive language: Focus on the strengths of your athletes and encourage them with positive words. Instead of saying, "Don't miss the pass," say, "Let's work on receiving the ball more accurately."

3. Speak at a level that suits their age and understanding: Tailor your messages based on the developmental level of your athletes. Don't talk down to them—but don't go over their heads, either.

4. Be careful with your tone: The way you say something often carries more weight than what you say. Always speak with a calm and respectful tone.

5.3. Leveraging Non-Verbal Communication

Non-verbal communication, like facial expressions, gestures, and body language, can complement or contradict your verbal messages. However, young athletes can miss subtle non-verbal cues. Consequently, being explicit and deliberate with your non-verbal communication goes a long way.

1. Pay attention to your facial expressions: A smile can make your athletes feel comfortable, while a furrowed brow could indicate disappointment or dissatisfaction.

2. Use gestures: Coaches often use hand signals, especially in loud settings. Teach your athletes these signals and use them consistently.

3. Maintain good posture: Your body language affects your authority and credibility. Standing tall and maintaining eye contact shows you are engaged and confident.

5.4. Active Listening: Hear and Understand

Communication is not just about talking—it's also about listening. Active listening involves fully understanding and responding appropriately to your athletes.

1. Show interest: Show that you're interested in what your athletes are saying. This action fosters open communication and shows them that their voices matter.

2. Avoid interrupting: Allow your athletes to finish speaking before you respond. This act shows respect for their opinions, even if you disagree with them.

3. Repeat and clarify: To ensure you've understood correctly, repeat back to them what you think you heard. Ask for clarification if needed.

5.5. Transforming Feedback into FeedForward

While coaching young athletes, it's important to focus not just on what they're doing wrong but also on what they can do in the future to improve. This concept, known as FeedForward, is a more positive approach to feedback.

1. Make feedback specific: Instead of general comments, provide specific instructions on what needs to be done. For instance, "You need more strength in your shots" could become, "Work on your wrist flick when you shoot for a better impact."

2. Focus on the future: Instead of dwelling on their past mistakes, discuss what they can do differently next time.

3. Keep feedback balanced: Make sure to give a healthy mix of positive comments (what they did right) and FeedForward (what they can work on).

5.6. Creating a Culture of Open Communication

Your role as a coach isn't only to improve physical capabilities, but also to foster a supportive and open atmosphere for communication within the team.

1. Promote team meetings: Regular team meetings are a great way to communicate collectively. Encourage open conversations and value each team member's contribution during these meetups.

2. Foster a safe and inclusive environment: Athletes should feel secure to voice their joys, fears, and concerns. This culture can be developed by treating everyone equally, irrespective of their gender, race, ability, or social background.

3. Encourage peer feedback: Young athletes can learn a lot from each other. Encourage them to share constructive feedback with their peers in a respectful manner.

5.7. The Art of Emotional Communication

A crucial yet often overlooked aspect of communication is

recognizing and responding appropriately to emotions. This skill, known as emotional intelligence, can help you foster an environment of empathetic communication.

1. Understand your own emotions: Being mindful of your emotions when you communicate allows you to control your reactions better.

2. Recognize your athletes' emotions: Pay attention to emotional cues—body language, tone of voice—from your athletes. This awareness will help you better understand how they are feeling.

3. Respond appropriately: Once you understand their feelings, respond in a manner that validates their emotions while gently guiding them towards a solution.

In conclusion, effective communication is indispensable for coaching young athletes. By consistently implementing these strategies, you can create a positive environment that brings out the best in each athlete and instills in them the true spirit of sportsmanship and joy.

Chapter 6. Building a Positive Team Culture

Establishing a positive team culture must be a top priority for any coach. It significantly influences a young athlete's experience, teaching them how to work together, respect each other, strive for excellence, and push individual limits. The essence of a positive team culture lies in team spirit, support, grit, resilience, sportsmanship, and the joy of playing the sport.

6.1. Defining a Clear Vision

A clear vision is a guiding force for any team. As a coach, you should establish the purpose and direction for the team. This could be to play the sport with discipline and respect, improve individual skills, or learn the importance of team dynamics. Ensure that each athlete understands this vision and its importance. Hold a meeting at the start of the season, laying out your vision, discussing it, and explaining how it will help each individual and the team as a whole. Make sure that your vision is systematically communicated, so that everyone is on the same page, facilitating smooth implementation of strategies.

6.2. Strong Coach-Leadership

An integral part of establishing a positive team culture is through solid coach leadership. Set the tone for your team by modeling positive behavior, fairness, and commitment to the sport. Players reflect the values and attitudes of their coach, making your role as a mentor quite influential. Be keenly aware of your actions and interactions with players and respond to situations in a manner that respects every individual's feelings and dignity. Above all, foster a coaching style that promotes learning, enjoyment, and competition.

6.3. Fostering Communication

Promote an open line of communication among all team members, including players, parents, and staff. Emphasize the importance of clear, respectful dialogue. Create a safe environment for players to express their feelings, thoughts, and ideas. Regular team meetings can be beneficial for sharing strategies, discussing issues, and brainstorming solutions. Clarity and openness in communication help avoid misunderstandings and provide collective direction.

6.4. Encouraging Teamwork and Collaboration

Teamwork makes the dream work, as the saying goes. The importance of this cannot be overstated in sports. Encourage collaboration by organizing team-building exercises, group tasks, and activities that require cooperation and joint effort. Develop a sense of camaraderie through shared experiences and goals. Ensure everyone understands the essential role they play in the team's success and underscore the significance of their contributions.

6.5. Highlighting Personal and Team Goals

Define a set of personal and team goals for the season, which can serve as stepping stones to success. Individual goals empower each player to focus on improving specific skills, while team goals promote collective ambition. By achieving these smaller, measurable goals, players will develop a sense of accomplishment, boosting their confidence and reinforcing the team's unity. Regularly review these goals and maintain a positive, supportive attitude in the face of setbacks.

6.6. Developing Resilience

In sports, setbacks and failures are as common as victories and successes, if not more so. Cultivate a culture that views these setbacks as opportunities for learning and development. Teach young athletes to recognize the significance of resilience and persistence. Celebrate efforts as much as outcomes, reinforcing that mistakes, when approached rightly, become stepping stones to success.

6.7. Promoting Sportsmanship

Sportsmanship is an essential aspect of any sports team. Encourage your players to respect their opponents, win or lose, and to value fair play above everything else. Sportsmanship also implies treating referees, teammates, and coaches with respect, appreciating their efforts and dedication. These lessons extend beyond the playing field, instilling values that will serve players well throughout life.

6.8. Celebrating Success and Learning from Failure

Make it a habit to celebrate success - be it a triumphant win or small individual achievements. Recognition, applause, or even just a pat on the back can greatly increase motivation and boost confidence. Similarly, recognize and handle failure effectively. Teach your players that failure is not the end but an opportunity to learn, grow, and become stronger.

In summation, building a positive team culture is a multifaceted endeavor. Incorporating these strategies will ensure your team not only performs well but also enjoys the journey, promoting lifelong skills and values. Remember, as a coach, your responsibility is not just to guide athletes in the sport, but to shape well-rounded individuals who understand the significance of respect, resilience, teamwork, and sportsmanship.

Chapter 7. Strengths-Based Coaching: Identifying and Utilizing Individual Player Strengths

One of the most powerful ways to motivate and engage young athletes is by employing a strengths-based approach to coaching. This approach does not focus on eradicating weaknesses but, in contrast, zeros in on identifying, developing, and utilizing the unique strengths of each player to optimize team performance. Let's dive deeply into understanding the philosophy, tools, and techniques of this compelling coaching strategy.

7.1. Understanding Strengths-Based Coaching

Primarily, it's crucial to understand what strengths-based coaching entails. In the realm of sports coaching, this signifies a shift from the conventional deficit-focused approach, which accentuates players' shortcomings and areas for improvement. The strengths-based approach is instead about tapping into each player's innate strengths, talents, and abilities and leveraging them to enhance their performance and that of the team. This method enables you to build a team where everyone is not only competent but excels in their individual roles.

7.2. Recognizing Player Strengths

Player strengths present themselves in various forms - physical strength, agility, speed, stamina, technical skills, game sense, leadership abilities, and mental resilience, among others. Identifying them requires keen observation, open dialogue, and even formal testing.

It's not about making snap judgments; it's about watching players over time, in different situations, and under varying degrees of pressure. There are multiple ways of identifying individual strengths:

1. Player-Self Analysis: Have the athletes rate their skills to get an idea of their perceived strengths. self-analysis encourages players to be self-aware of their abilities.

2. Peer Evaluation: Your players' teammates can provide valuable insights into strengths you may not see as the coach. Encourage players to offer constructive feedback to each other.

3. Standard Tests: In some sports like basketball or soccer, standardized tests can help measure physical or technical strengths like speed, strength or accuracy.

4. Coach Observation: Your observations as a coach can sometimes be the most valuable. Watch your players during training and games and make notes on their standout areas.

7.3. Developing Strengths

No matter how innate, strengths need to be nurtured. Here are some strategies to guide further development:

1. Individualized Training Plans: Design plans that align with each player's strengths. This requires tailoring specific drills, activities, and exercises to emphasize and enhance these strengths.

2. Constructive Feedback: Use feedback sessions to reinforce positive aspects of a player's performance. Make sure to express praise in a specific and sincere manner to motivate athletes.

3. Exposure: Provide opportunities for players to display and refine their strengths during games and practices. This not only

develops the players but also boosts their confidence.

7.4. Building a Strengths-Based Team

Harmonizing individual strengths to form a cohesive unit is key to a successful team:

1. Role Assignment: Assign roles based on each player's strengths. This optimizes team performance by ensuring tasks are carried out by those most proficient at them.

2. Team Synergy: Balance the different strengths so that they complement each other. This interplay can create a harmonious team dynamic, making your team more formidable.

3. Reciprocal Learning: Encourage players to learn from each other. This way, they can not only improve on their weaknesses but also enhance their strengths by learning from peers who excel in particular areas.

7.5. Navigating Challenges

Strengths-based coaching isn't without challenges. It may lead to players developing a one-dimensional outlook if not guided properly. Balance strengths development with overall skills enhancement to prevent this. Additionally, maintaining fair treatment and avoiding favoritism is essential when focusing on individual strengths. All players should feel their unique strengths are valued.

Adopting a strengths-based approach will empower you and your team, creating an environment where performance, motivation, and satisfaction all improve. Remember, the focus is not solely on winning games, but in supporting young athletes to reach their highest potential. By leveraging their strengths, you nurture their journey in sports, encourage a lifelong love for the game, and construct a formidable team that celebrates each other's triumphs, creating a legacy of success.

Chapter 8. Tackling Challenges: Handling Losses and Overcoming Obstacles

While it's true that the sweet smell of victory inspires and motivates, losses and obstacles are just as pivotal in shaping the growth of our young athletes. By handling these challenges correctly, we can turn every game, irrespective of the outcome, into an enriching learning experience.

8.1. The Psychological Impact of Loss

Losing is an inevitable part of sports. No one wins all the time, not even seasoned professionals. However, wayward emotions and dampened motivation can affect young athletes in the wake of defeat. Players may experience frustration, disappointment, decreased self-esteem, and increased anxiety, all of which can diminish their love for the game. As a coach, it is essential to understand the psychological implications of losses and use them as building blocks for both personal and team growth.

There are several key strategies to help young athletes cope with and overcome the psychological impact of loss:

- Show Empathy: Encourage them to express their feelings about the loss and assure them it's okay to feel disappointed.

- Emphasis on Effort: Highlight their efforts and the positives in their play, rather than focusing on the result.

- Set Goals: Discuss areas of improvement and set actionable goals for next games.

- Teach Resilience: Arm them with the understanding that failures are stepping stones to success.

8.2. The Role of Resilience in Overcoming Obstacles

Resilience is key to overcoming obstacles and coming back stronger from losses. It is about learning to bounce back and adapt in the face of adversity. Here's how to build resilience in young athletes:

- Encourage a Growth Mindset: Teach your team that skills can be developed and mastered over time through hard work and consistent practice.

- Encourage Problem-Solving: Instill a never-give-up attitude and inspire them to find solutions, rather than surrendering to adversity.

- Bring in Role Models: Young players can learn resilience by hearing about sports personalities who have faced and overcome significant obstacles.

- Provide Support: A supportive environment can foster resilience. Let your players know you are there to help them navigate through their sporting journey.

8.3. Defeat as a Learning Experience

An experienced coach views defeat not as failure, but as a virtuous cycle of learning, adjustment, and development. Here's how you can make this shift:

- Debrief and Analyze: Review the game with your team and discuss what went wrong, what went right, and what could be improved.

- Streamline Training: Tailor subsequent training sessions based on weaknesses and areas of improvement identified in the game analysis.

- Praise Improvement: Recognize and celebrate individual and team improvements, no matter how small.

Taking these steps in the aftermath of a loss can convert defeat into an opportunity for understanding and improvement.

8.4. Nurturing a Growth Mindset

Adopting a growth mindset is a key to turning obstacles into opportunities. To cultivate this in your players:

- Reinforce the Idea of 'Yet': Remind players that they might not be good at something 'yet', but they will become proficient over time with consistent efforts.

- Show that Errors are Part of Learning: Teach them that making errors is a part of the process, and they can learn from them.

- Celebrate Progress, Not Just Outcomes: Encourage progress by recognizing skill developments and improvements in their game over time.

With a growth mindset, players start to focus on development rather than on wins and losses.

8.5. Formulating a Constructive Action Plan

Having a comprehensive plan to address challenges and ensure steady progress can ease the journey for both coaches and players. This plan should entail the following steps:

- Identifying the Challenges: Clearly recognizing the obstacles faced by players clarifies the path to improvement.

- Creating Tailored Strategies: Devise effective strategies that correspond to individual players' needs and challenges.

- Implementing the Plan: Ensure the plan's elements are integrated into your coaching and training sessions.

- Review and Adjust: Regularly evaluate your plan's effectiveness. Adjust as required based on results and progress.

Remember, the act of losing does not make a player a loser. Rather, the response to that loss defines who they are as players and individuals. Managing losses and adversity effectively can turn these seemingly negative experiences into positive ones, fostering growth, resilience, and a love for the game that will carry our young athletes through their sporting journeys and beyond.

Chapter 9. The Ethics of Sports: Instilling Fair Play and Sportsmanship

Teaching children about the ethics of sportsmanship is one of the most critical responsibilities bestowed upon a youth sports coach. Instilling these principles early on shapes not only the athlete but the person behind the athlete. It involves emphasizing fair play, respect for the game, and the significance of character over victory.

9.1. Fair Play

Playing fair is an integral part of sports and is central to teaching kids about ethics in sports. It means adhering to the rules, being respectful of other players, and putting one's best effort into the game.

Fair play begins with understanding the rules of the game. Coaches should take time to explain these rules thoroughly. Each session can incorporate a 'Rule of the Day,' affording players the chance to learn and apply when necessary.

Training sessions should focus on promoting fairness by prioritizing skill development over winning. Through drills that encourage fair play, children can learn the importance of playing clean, avoiding foul plays, and being honest in their actions. Practicing these skills will instill a sense of integrity in young athletes that extends beyond the field.

9.2. Respect for Opponents

A crucial side of sports ethics is respect for competitors. It teaches children they should regard every opponent as an equal, irrespective of their skill level. This respect should reflect in their behavior both on and off the field.

To cultivate respect for opponents, coaches can use team discussions to talk about successful sports figures known for their exemplary behavior. Additionally, regular reinforcement of positive attitudes during matches can shift the focus from winning at any cost to valifying the opponent's efforts.

Coaches can also organize friendly matches with the philosophy 'compete, not defeat.' Such a mindset stresses the importance of competition over winning, fostering respect for the opponent's abilities.

9.3. Team Spirit

Team spirit is an integral part of sportsmanship. It goes beyond encouraging your team; it involves appreciating every member's contribution and displaying respect towards teammates, coaches, and opponents.

To cultivate team spirit, use exercises that require team dynamics to succeed. Activities stressing cooperation over individual achievement help young athletes understand that everyone's contribution matters and that a team's strength lies in unity.

Recognition of effort and good sportsmanship can be just as important as praising athletic skill. Reward systems that acknowledge attitude, effort, and fair play can cultivate an environment where team spirit thrives.

9.4. Building Character Over Winning

A good sports coach knows the score at the end of the game isn't all that matters. The real win lies in the character development the players undergo during their sporting journey.

Emphasize the character-building aspects of sports. Teach them lessons about perseverance, humility, discipline, and resilience that sport inherently offers. Holding post-match discussions about handling a win or a loss, the exertion of effort, and individual growth can instill values that last long after leaving the field.

The peculiar thing about sports is that it doesn't necessarily build character; it reveals it. Encourage them to be just as gracious in victory as they are in defeat.

9.5. Dealing with Victory and Defeat

The ability to handle both victory and defeat graciously is a fundamental skill young athletes should master. It teaches children about acceptance, humility, and growth.

When discussing victory, emphasize the importance of humility. Winners should learn to acknowledge their opponents' efforts and offer appreciation for a game well-played.

Conversely, children must understand that defeat is not a failure but an opportunity for learning. Encourage them to identify what they did well and what needs improvement. The primary goal is to convey that losing is not the end of the world, but rather a stepping stone towards success.

By highlighting the learnings from each win or loss, you ensure that the focus of play is not solely on the outcome, but the journey taken to get there.

Sports ethics goes far beyond the playing field—it plays a significant role in shaping young individuals in their journey of growth and character building. Teaching sportsmanship helps children understand the values of fair play, respect, and humility. As a coach, remember, every session, every match is a stepping stone towards not only creating good athletes but good human beings.

Chapter 10. Fitness and Health: Ensuring Proper Exercise and Nutrition

Physical fitness and healthy nutrition are two critical aspects that contribute significantly to the well-being and performance of young athletes. These foundations ensure their bodies can endure rigorous training, provide them with energy, and condition their physique to reduce the risk of injuries. Coaches should make it their mission to emphasize these aspects and help athletes understand their importance.

10.1. Exercise Functionality and Appropriateness for Age

Young bodies are still developing physically and thus require a different approach to exercise when compared to adults. According to the National Strength and Conditioning Association, resistance training for children can be safe and effective if the coach ensures the programs are age-appropriate and supervised by well-qualified adults.

A balanced exercise program for young athletes should entail a variety of activities to promote overall physical development. It should contain aerobic exercises like running, biking, or swimming, strengthening exercises like push-ups and squats, and flexibility exercises such as stretches. Instruct athletes to perform each movement correctly, ensuring proper form to decrease the risk of injury.

Safety should always come first. As the body matures, the exercises may become more complex, but the fundamentals remain the same:

a balanced approach with an emphasis on safety. Incorporating fun into drills and practices can maintain the interest and enthusiasm of the players in this essential aspect of their overall development.

10.2. Healthy Nutritional Habits

Proper nutrition is as important as exercise in the development of a young athlete. The three major macronutrients: carbohydrates, protein, and fats, play unique roles in providing energy and building blocks for growth and recovery.

Carbohydrates are the body's primary source of energy and are critical for high-intensity athletic performance. Whole grains, fruits, and vegetables are excellent sources of healthy carbohydrates.

Protein, on the other hand, is crucial for tissue repair and muscle growth. Sources include lean meats, poultry, fish, beans, and dairy products.

Lastly, despite common misconceptions, fats are essential for hormonal balance, brain function, and as a slow-burning energy source. Healthy sources of fat include avocados, nuts, seeds, and fatty fish like salmon.

While educating young athletes about the importance of nutrition is crucial, it is equally important to foster a healthy relationship with food. Teach them the value of balanced eating rather than promoting strict diets.

10.3. Hydration

Water plays an important role in the physiological function and performance enhancement of athletes. Encourage players to hydrate before, during, and after physical activity. Also, teach them the signs of dehydration such as dry mouth, lack of energy, and lightheadedness.

Every coach must understand that each athlete is different and hydration needs might vary significantly, depending on factors like age, weight, and intensity of activity. A flexible approach is essential to individual hydration needs.

10.4. Rest and Recovery

An often overlooked, but critical aspect of sport participation, rest and recovery are essential for the growth, performance, and injury prevention for youth athletes. Sleep enables the body to repair itself, consolidate memory, and flush out toxins. Encourage athletes to prioritize good sleep hygiene habits.

Additionally, incorporate regular periods of lighter activity and complete rest into the training schedule. This down time may reduce the prevalence of overuse injuries and help prevent burnout.

In conclusion, the role of a youth sports coach is not only to develop athletes' skills, but also to ensure their health and well-being. A comprehensive approach that includes proper exercise, nutrition, hydration, and rest is critical in the journey of growing a young athlete. Remember, a healthier athlete is a more effective and resilient athlete.

Coaching is an opportunity to make a lifetime impact. By developing comprehensive strategies that prioritize health and fitness, you're not just developing better athletes: you're shaping healthier individuals.

Chapter 11. Keeping it Fun: Ensuring an Enjoyable Experience for Young Athletes

At the core of youth sports is the goal to make the experience enjoyable for young athletes. Keeping the fun factor isn't always as simple as it seems, but it's the key to a rewarding experience for both the players and the coach.

11.1. Understanding the Importance of Fun

In the world of youth sports, the element of fun is an often-underestimated motivational tool. While the notion of competition and striving for excellence remain significantly important, maintaining a fun environment plays a crucial role in keeping young athletes engaged and developing their skills.

Research shows that fun is the main reason children participate in sports. When they enjoy participating, they're more likely to stick with it, continue to practice, and ultimately make improvements. Conversely, too much pressure and emphasis on winning can decrease their enjoyment, leading to burnout or premature departure from the sport.

11.2. Fun Vs. Winning: Striking the Right Balance

Coaching youth sports isn't just about teaching the technical aspects of the game. It's about creating an atmosphere that encourages enjoyment and fosters overall development. One major pitfall to avoid is losing sight of the primary goal - facilitating a love for the sport - and focusing too intensely on winning.

Winning can be fun, but it shouldn't be the only measure of success. Kids should be learning new skills, improving existing ones, and gaining experience in teamwork and sportsmanship. As a coach, make sure to celebrate these accomplishments, not just the final score.

11.3. How to Incorporate Fun into Practice

Making practice sessions fun holds the key to maintain high interest and engagement levels among young athletes. The following strategies can help:

1. Incorporate games: Introduce games that refine fundamental skills, promote team spirit, and induce a sense of delight. Keep an element of surprise to keep players guessing and fostering enthusiasm.

2. Rewarding system: Create a system of rewards that brings moments of joy to players for their hard work, improvement, sportsmanship, and other values. These awards need not be materialistic; they can be simple recognitions that boost players' morale.

3. Mix it up: Avoid monotony by bringing in diversity in the training plans. This could include different drills, locations for training, or even a surprise day of fun activities unrelated to the sport.

4. Use Humor: A joke or a funny story can instantly lift the mood and diffuse tension. This can be especially helpful on tough practice days or after a loss.

11.4. The Role of a Positive Attitude

The disposition of a coach plays a significant role in shaping the squad's overall experience. A positive attitude from the coach creates an uplifting environment that encourages players to give their best while not losing the essence of fun. Here's how to use a positive outlook to create a playful atmosphere:

- Leadership Style: Guiding players on the field rather than authoritative commands enables youth to explore, take risks, make mistakes, learn, and grow.

- Failure is OK: Make it safe for players to fail. They need to know that making mistakes is a part of learning, and it's alright if they don't succeed every time.

- Positive Affirmation: Regularly validating players' efforts goes a long way. Ensure to offer positive feedback whenever you get a chance.

11.5. Fun-Led Performance: A Winning Strategy

Contrary to popular belief, keeping things fun can lead to excellent performances on the field. When players are enjoying what they are doing, they tend to perform better. The decrease in pressure allows more room for creativity, and a fun environment can raise the players' motivation to practice, both of which contribute to enhancing performance.

In conclusion, increasing the fun factor in youth sports isn't just about making the environment more enjoyable – though that certainly matters. It also promotes team cohesion, lowers drop-out rates, enhances skill development, and can lead to better match-day performances. A coach who can make sports fun for the young athletes is setting them up for lasting success in any venture they pursue.

Remember, you don't just want to coach young athletes for the game - you want to coach them for life. Keeping it fun is one of the best ways to do just that. After all, a love for the sport is the best appetizer for a lifelong journey of physical fitness, camaraderie, and valuable life lessons learned on the field of play.